SLAVE ISLAND
&
THE COLONY

two utopian comedies

Pierre Carlet de Marivaux

Translated from French by
Laurence Senelick

BROADWAY PLAY PUBLISHING INC
New York
www.broadwayplaypub.com
info@broadwayplaypub.com

Cover illustration: *Harlequin and His Lady* by Giovanni Domenico Ferretti (1692-1768)

First edition: October 2021
I S B N: 978-0-88145-911-1

Book design: Marie Donovan
Page make-up: Adobe InDesign
Typeface: Palatino

INTRODUCTION

Pierre Carlet de Chamblain de Marivaux (1688-1763), scion of a wealthy and noble family, lost his fortune in 1722 and turned to writing to earn a living. He began as a journalist, editing *Le Spectateur français*, became a fixture in Paris salons and in 1742 was admitted to the Académie Française. The greatest comic French author between Molière and Beaumarchais, Marivaux created a new genre, the comedy of feeling, in plays written between 1721 and 1741 for the Théâtre Italien in Paris. Its actors were transplanted *commedia dell' arte* players and he adapted their traditions to embody his own dramatic concepts. Their masked and disguised comedians were rendered more recognizably human with complicated emotions. Marivaux moved French comedy from Molière's world of sharply outlined types to the "psychology" of love, which had previously been sidelined in *commedia* or demoted to a plot device. The German critic Lessing called Marivaux's innovation a "metaphysical dissection of the passions," while Diderot coined the term "marivaudage" to characterize his bantering dialogue.

The framework of fairy tale, allegory or what the French call Robinsonade (being cast away on a desert island, like Robinson Crusoe) provides a contrast for the reality of the characters' states of mind. In *L'Île des esclaves* (SLAVE ISLAND) and *La Colonie* (THE COLONY), the concrete problems of Marivaux's time—nature vs culture, the critique of social institutions and structures, class and gender equality—are played out before an abstract background.

SLAVE ISLAND was first produced on Monday, 5 March 1725 by Lelio Riccoboni's troupe and the Comédie-Italienne at the Hôtel de Bourgogne, Paris. It was such a success that it ran for an unheard-of twenty performances in a row, and its notoriety made it the talk of the town. On 18 June 1725, Marivaux followed it with a three-act comedy *La Nouvelle Colonie (The New Colony)* also at the Comédie-Italienne. It met with a cold reception and closed the next day. In December 1750 Marivaux published a revision in one act called *The Colony* in the *Mercure de France*. It is believed to have been performed once or twice on the private stage of the Comte de Clermont. Both plays have enjoyed frequent revivals, especially in France and the U K, in the last twenty-five years. Their themes have renewed relevance and make Marivaux seem especially prescient in matters of gender and class, slavery and colonialism.

SLAVE ISLAND
(*L'ÎLE DES ESCLAVES*—1725)

CHARACTERS & SETTING

IPHICRATES
HARLEQUIN
EUPHROSYNE
CLEANTHIS
TRIVELIN
ISLANDERS *(non-speaking roles which may easily be cut)*

The action takes place on Slave Island. The stage represents a sea and boulders on one side and on the other a few trees and houses.

(IPHICRATES *moves down in a dejected attitude and crosses the stage with* HARLEQUIN.)

IPHICRATES: *(After a sigh)* Harlequin!

HARLEQUIN: *(A bottle of wine slung from his belt)* Boss!

IPHICRATES: What's to become of us on this island?

HARLEQUIN: Become of us? Skin and bones, living skeletons, slow death by starvation. That's how I'm feeling right now and that's what's staring us in the face.

IPHICRATES: We are the only ones who escaped the shipwreck. All our friends have perished, and now I envy their fate.

HARLEQUIN: Sorry to say! They drowned in the sea and we're up to our necks in it.

IPHICRATES: Remember! When our ship broke upon the rocks, some of our shipmates had time to jump into the lifeboat. But then the waves swallowed it up. I don't know what happened next but maybe they were lucky enough to wash up somewhere on this island. I think we ought to search for them.

HARLEQUIN: Search for 'em, not a bad idea. But first let's rest a bit and down a little brandy. I managed to rescue my poor bottle here. I'll drink two thirds, which is only fair, and then I'll let you have what's left.

IPHICRATES: Hey! There's no time to waste. Follow me. We must leave no stone unturned to get out of this place. If I'm don't manage to escape, I'm doomed. I'll never see Athens again, for we've been cast ashore on Slave Island.

HARLEQUIN: Oho! What sort of tribe lives here?

IPHICRATES: They're Greek slaves who rose up against their masters a hundred years ago and came to settle on an island. I think it's this very one. Look, those are probably some of their huts. Their custom, my dear Harlequin, is to kill all the masters they come across or else make slaves of them.

HARLEQUIN: Huh! Each country has its own way of doing things. They kill masters, fine and dandy. The way I heard it slaves like me they leave alone.

IPHICRATES: True enough.

HARLEQUIN: So what! We're still alive and kicking.

IPHICRATES: But I'm in danger of losing my liberty and perhaps my life. Harlequin, isn't that reason enough to feel for me?

HARLEQUIN: *(Taking the bottle and taking a swig)* Ah! I feel for you from the bottom of my…my heart, fair enough.

IPHICRATES: Then follow me.

HARLEQUIN: Hoo! Hoo! Hoo!

IPHICRATES: What's that supposed to mean?

HARLEQUIN: *(Carelessly sings)* Tala ta lara.

IPHICRATES: Talk sense. Have you lost your mind? What's the meaning of this?

HARLEQUIN: *(Laughing)* Ha, ha, ha! Master Iphicrates, it's funny the way things turn out! I do feel for you, honest I do, but I can't help laughing.

IPHICRATES: *(Aside at first)* The rascal is enjoying my life-threatening situation. I should never have told him where we are. Harlequin, this is no time or place for your high jinks. Let's go in that direction.

HARLEQUIN: My legs have fallen asleep!

IPHICRATES: Let's be on our way, if you don't mind.

HARLEQUIN: If you don't mind, if you don't mnd. How polite and civil of you. Must be the local climate.

IPHICRATES: Move it, step on it, just half a mile over that way we might locate our lifeboat. Maybe we'll find some of our shipmates; and then we can get back on board.

HARLEQUIN: *(Jesting)* Funny fellow! The things you come up with! *(He sings.)*
To steer a ship takes lots of spunk;
The rocking makes me woozy.
I'd rather be snug in my bunk,
Cavorting with some floozy.

IPHICRATES: *(Restraining his anger)* Sometimes I can't figure you out, my dear Harlequin.

HARLEQUIN: My dear boss, I can't get over this flow of compliments. Usually you thump me with a cudgel and that's not half so nice. But the cudgel is in the lifeboat.

IPHICRATES: Hey! Don't you know how fond I am of you?

HARLEQUIN: Yes; but your fondness always leaves its love-bites on my backside, which suggests poor aim. And, listen, about our shipmates, it's out of our hands! If they're dead, what's the rush? If they're alive, it's only a matter of time, and I'll drink to that!

IPHICRATES: *(Quite upset)* But I need their help.

HARLEQUIN: *(Casually)* Oh! no doubt about that. That's your worry. I won't stand in your way!

IPHICRATES: Insolent slave!

HARLEQUIN: Aha! Now you're speaking the language of Athens, a vulgar lingo I don't savvy.

IPHICRATES: Don't you know I'm your master? Aren't you still my slave?

HARLEQUIN: (*Moving away, seriously*) I was once, I confess it to your shame, but, there, I forgive you. Some people just aren't worth the bother. In the land of Athens, I was your slave. You treated me like a dumb animal, and you said it was only right and proper, because you had the upper hand. All right then! Iphicrates, around here you'll find they've got a higher upper hand than you do. They'll enslave you in turn. And then they'll tell you it's only right and proper, and we'll see what you think of such rightness. I can't wait to hear how it makes you feel. Once you've suffered, you'll learn more sense. You'll have a clearer picture of how some of us suffer at the hands of others. It would be a much better world if all your sort were taught the same lesson. Farewell, my friend; I'm going to find my comrades and your masters. (*He moves some distance away.*)

IPHICRATES: (*In despair, running after him, sword in hand*) Good heavens! Can a man be more miserable, more sinned against than I am? Wretch! You don't deserve to live.

HARLEQUIN: Take it easy. You've lost your powers, I won't come when called, so mind your manners!

(TRIVELIN *and five or six* ISLANDERS *enter escorting a* LADY *and her* MAID-SERVANT. *The* ISLANDERS *run to* IPHICRATES *when they see he is holding a sword.*)

TRIVELIN: (*has his men seize and disarm* IPHICRATES) Stop, what do you think you're doing?

IPHICRATES: Punishing my slave's insolence.

TRIVELIN: Your slave! You're wrong about that and you'll be taught to keep a civil tongue in your head.

(TRIVELIN *takes* IPHICRATES' *sword and gives it to* HARLEQUIN.)

TRIVELIN: Take this sword, comrade. It is yours.

HARLEQUIN: A long life to you, old pal!

TRIVELIN: What is your name?

HARLEQUIN: My name?

TRIVELIN: Yes, your name.

HARLEQUIN: I don't have one, comrade.

TRIVELIN: What, you don't have a name?

HARLEQUIN: No, comrade. They only call me by pet names. Sometimes Harlequin, sometimes Hey You.

TRIVELIN: Hey You! That's an insult. These gentlemen are notorious for taking such liberties. And him, has he got a name?

HARLEQUIN: Oh, sure! He's got a name all right. It's Lord Iphicrates.

TRIVELIN: Well! swap names for now. Be Lord Iphicrates in turn and your name, Iphicrates, is now Harlequin alias Hey You.

HARLEQUIN: (*Jumping for joy; to his master*) Oh, oh! that's a laugh, Lord Hey You!

TRIVELIN: (*To* HARLEQUIN) Take care now you bear his name, dear friend. It has been given you not to stoke your vanity but to wound his pride.

HARLEQUIN: Yes, yes, wounding, I'm all for wounding!

IPHICRATES: (*Glaring at* HARLEQUIN) You knave!

HARLEQUIN: Look at that, pal, he's taking another liberty. Can he get away with that?

TRIVELIN: *(To* HARLEQUIN*)* For the moment, he can say whatever he wants to you. *(To* IPHICRATES*)* Harlequin, you're in a difficult situation, and you feel that Iphicrates and I are treating you badly. Don't let it get to you, relieve your feelings by losing your temper. Call him a wretch and us as well. You're free to do so for now; but, once the probation period is over, bear in mind that you are Harlequin, he is Iphicrates, and you are to him what he was once to you. These are the laws of our republic and it's my job to see that this community observes them.

HARLEQUIN: Ah! a pretty cushy job!

IPHICRATES: Me, slave to this lowlife!

TRIVELIN: He once was yours.

HARLEQUIN: It's not so hard! So long as the fellow obeys my every whim, I'll treat 'im to all sorts of goodies.

IPHICRATES: So I'm allowed to say whatever I please. That's not enough. Let me have a big stick as well.

HARLEQUIN: Comrade, he's aiming to address my backside. For the time being, I place it under the protection of the republic,

TRIVELIN: Have no fear.

CLEANTHIS: *(To* TRIVELIN*)* Sir, I am a slave as well, and off the same ship. Please don't forget about me.

TRIVELIN: No, my dear child. The way you are dressed revealed your position. I was just about to deal with you when I saw the sword in his hand. Let me finish what I have to say to Harlequin!

HARLEQUIN: *(Thinking* TRIVELIN *refers to him)* Right!… Oops, I'm supposed to be Iphicrates.

TRIVELIN: *(Proceeding)* Keep it straight. You know who we are, I suppose?

HARLEQUIN: Oh! sure! Kind-hearted people.

CLEANTHIS: Who mean us well.

TRIVELIN: No interruptions, children. I think you do know who we are. Our forefathers, exasperated by their masters' cruelty and resenting the atrocities they suffered at the hands of their owners, fled Greece and came to settle here. The first law they passed was that any slave-owner brought to their island by chance or shipwreck would be put to death, and any slave set free. Vengeance dictated that law. Twenty years later cooler heads repealed it, and legislated a milder one. We no longer wreak revenge on you, we correct you. We do not wish to take your life, but to root out the inhumanity in your hearts. We force you into slavery to make you aware of the evils it entails. We humiliate you so that you will reproach yourselves for being arrogant. Your bondage, or rather your lesson in humanity, will last three years, at the end of which time you will be sent home if your masters are satisfied with your progress. And, if you show no improvement, we shall house you out of charity to keep you from oppressing others somewhere else. Out of our concern for you, we shall marry you off to one of our fellow-citizens. Such are our laws in this regard. Appreciate their rigor and take full advantage of it. Thank fate for having brought you here. Harsh, unjust and arrogant you have come into our care. You're in a bad way now, but we undertake to cure you. You are not so much our slaves as our patients. A mere three years should be enough to effect a cure and make you humane, reasonable and tolerant for the rest of your lives.

HARLEQUIN: And all at no extra charge, without enemas or leeches. Can you get medical coverage cheaper than that?

TRIVELIN: By the way, don't try to escape these parts, you will fail in the attempt and make your situation even worse. Begin your new way of life with patience.

HARLEQUIN: How can he possibly object since it's for his own good?

TRIVELIN: *(To* HARLEQUIN *and* CLEANTHIS*)* As for you, children, you are free citizens. You, Iphicrates, will live in this hut with the new Harlequin, and this fair maid shall dwell in the other. You must see about exchanging clothes, it is customary.

*(*IPHICRATES *exits into the hut.)*

TRIVELIN: *(To* HARLEQUIN*)* If you're hungry, go to that house over there and you'll be given something to eat. You must also be informed that you have a week to celebrate your change of status. After that you will be given a suitable occupation, like everyone else. Go on, I shall await you here. *(To the* ISLANDERS.*)* Take them away. *(To the* WOMEN*)* You two, stay here.

*(*IPHICRATES, HARLEQUIN *and the* ISLANDERS *exit.* HARLEQUIN, *on his way out, bows elaborately to* CLEANTHIS.*)*

TRIVELIN: Now then! Fellow citizen—for from now on I consider our island as your home land—tell me your name as well.

CLEANTHIS: *(Curtseying)* My name is Cleanthis, and hers is Euphrosyne.

TRIVELIN: Cleanthis? That'll do for now.

CLEANTHIS: I have pet names too. Would you like to hear them?

TRIVELIN: Indeed I would. What are they?

CLEANTHIS: I've got a list: Fool. Butterfingers. Nitwit. Dummy, the list goes on and on.

EUPHROSYNE: *(With a sigh)* Saucy baggage!

CLEANTHIS: There, that's one I forgot.

TRIVELIN: Indeed, she has caught you in the act. In your country, Euphrosyne, it's easy to fling insults at those who can't answer back.

EUPHROSYNE: For heaven's sake! How am I supposed to talk to her now that I'm in this weird situation?

CLEANTHIS: Oh, so, now it's not so easy to find a snappy comeback. Once upon a time it couldn't be simpler. Dealing with the scum of the earth. Why make any bones about it? "Do this. Because I want it. Shut up, fool." And that was that. But now, a person has to speak politely. That's a foreign language for my lady. She'll learn it in time. We just have to be patient. I'll do my best to drill it into her.

TRIVELIN: *(To* CLEANTHIS*)* Easy does it, Euphrosyne. *(To* EUPHROSYNE*)* And you, Cleanthis, do not give way to your grief. I can neither change our laws nor make an exception of you. I have explained how excellent they are and meant for your own good.

CLEANTHIS: Huh! I'll be surprised if you see the least change in her.

TRIVELIN: But your sex is the weaker by nature. Hence, in your past life, you have yielded more easily than a man might to the temptation of being haughty, disdainful and unfeeling to your fellow-creatures. All I can do on your behalf is to beg Euphrosyne to overlook the wrongs you have done her and be fair when she weighs them up.

CLEANTHIS: Oh! listen, that's all too highfalutin for me, I can't make head or tail of it. I'll take the low road and weigh with my thumb on the scale, same as she did. If she ever wrongs me in future, we'll know what steps to take.

TRIVELIN: Gently pray, no wreaking revenge.

CLEANTHIS: But, dear friend, after all, you were the one who said "yours is the weaker sex." If being weak is her excuse, well then, it's mine too. I've not got the strength to forgive and forget. If I have to forgive all her bad behavior to me, then she'll have to forgive my resentment towards her; for I'm every inch the woman she is. Look here, who's in charge? Aren't I the mistress this time round? Well, let her start by forgiving my resentment; and then I'll forgive her what she's done to me, —when I'm feel up to it. She can wait!

EUPHROSYNE: *(To* TRIVELIN*)* What a thing to say! How long do I have to listen to this?

CLEANTHIS: Put up with it, my lady, your bad behavior's come back to haunt you.

TRIVELIN: Come, come, Euphrosyne, mind your temper.

CLEANTHIS: How do you expect me to talk? If you're angry, the best remedy is to let off steam, see? When I've knocked her around a dozen times as I see fit, we'll be even. But it's something I've got to do.

TRIVELIN: *(Aside, to* EUPHROSYNE*)* This will run its course; but be consoled, it will end sooner than you think. *(To* CLEANTHIS*)* I hope, Euphrosyne, that you will get over your resentment. I urge you to do so as a friend. Now let's move on to the analysis of her character. You are required to paint me a portrait of it, and it has to be done in the presence of the model, so she will come to know herself, blush at her affectations, if she has any, and reform. Our aims are well-intentioned, as you see. All right, let's begin.

CLEANTHIS: Oh! what a clever idea! All right, I'm ready. Fire away. I'm an old hand at this!

EUPHROSYNE: *(Meekly)* Please, sir, let me take my leave, so that I don't have to listen to what she's about to say.

TRIVELIN: Sorry! My dear lady, this is being staged for your benefit. You have to be present.

CLEANTHIS: Stay, stay. A little shame won't kill you.

TRIVELIN: Vain, simpering and flirtatious, that's a random sample of the qualities I have to ask about. Do they apply to her?

CLEANTHIS: Vain, simpering and flirtatious, do they apply to her? Ha! That's my darling mistress to the life. The spitten image.

EUPHROSYNE: There, isn't that enough, sir?

TRIVELIN: Ah! congratulations on feeling a little pang. You do care, that's a good sign, and a good portent for the future. But so far these are only broad strokes. Let's probe in detail. Where, for example, do you find those faults we speak of?

CLEANTHIS: Where? Everywhere, every time, every place. I said ask me questions, but where to begin? I haven't a clue, I'm at a loss. There's so much wrong with her, so much I've seen with my own eyes that things get mixed up. My lady may keep her mouth shut, my lady may choose to speak; she may look around, feel sad, cheer up. Silent, talkative, wide-eyed, sad, cheerful, it's all the same tone, only the shading's different. Her vanity may be unspoken or smug or irritable. Her flirting may be chatty or jealous or inquisitive. That's my lady, always vain or flirtatious, one or the other, or both at once. That's what she's like. There, not a bad start.

EUPHROSYNE: I can't stand it.

TRIVELIN: Wait a bit, this is only the beginning.

CLEANTHIS: My lady gets up in the morning. Has she enjoyed her beauty sleep? Has she had her forty winks, does she feel alert, with a sprightly glint in her eye? Quick, to arms: it's going to be a glorious day. "Bring me my clothes!" My lady plans to entertain company today. She plans to go to plays, walks in the park, get-togethers. Her face will be on display, it will brave bright sunlight, it will be a pleasure to look at, just trot it out boldly, it's in fine shape, there's nothing to fear.

TRIVELIN: *(To* EUPHROSYNE*)* She's getting the hang of this.

CLEANTHIS: Has my lady, on the other hand, slept badly? "Ah! bring me a mirror. What a state I'm in! I look a fright!" No matter how long she gazes at her reflection, no matter how much she screws up her face every which way, nothing works. Eyes haggard, complexion pasty. It's no use, that face has to be covered up, all we'll wear is a house coat, madam will see no one today, not even daylight, if possible. At the very least keep the room dark. Even so, company shows up, somebody drops by. What will they think of my lady's face? They'll assume she's turned ugly. Will she give her dear friends that satisfaction? No, there's a remedy for everything; you'll see. "How are you feeling today, madam?" "Not at all well, madam. I passed a sleepless night, I haven't had a bit of shut-eye for a week. I dare not show myself in public, I look horrid." Which means: "Gentlemen, keep in mind that this is not how I ordinarily look. Avert your eyes, try not to stare at me. Do not judge me today. Wait until I've had a good night's sleep." The reason I know all about it, we slaves, we're able to see right through our masters! …Oh! and we find them contemptible.

TRIVELIN: *(To* EUPHROSYNE*)* Bear up, madam. Profit by this portrait, for it seems to me a good likeness.

EUPHROSYNE: I don't know where to hide.

CLEANTHIS: You're two-thirds along; and I'll give it the finishing touch, to keep from boring you.

TRIVELIN: Do so, do so. My lady can easily put up with what's to come.

CLEANTHIS: Remember the night you were with that good-looking cavalry officer? I was in the room. You were conversing in whispers, but I've got sharp hearing. You wanted to seduce him without being obvious. You mentioned a woman he's often seen with. "That woman is so attractive," you were saying. "Her eyes may squint, but they're so expressive"; whereat you opened yours wide, lowered your voice, tilted your head, wriggled and jiggled. It made me laugh. Still, you did get your way, the officer fell into the trap. He offered you his heart. "For me?" you said. "Yes, madam, your very own self, the most adorable creature in this world." "Go on, you silly man, go on," you said, taking off your gloves with the excuse of asking me to fetch another pair. "But what a lovely hand you have." He sees it, takes it, kisses it. It prompts him to make you the proposition, and that was the gloves you were asking for. Well! have I hit the bull's eye?

TRIVELIN: (To EUPHROSYNE) Truly, she's right on target.

CLEANTHIS: Listen, listen, here's the funniest part. One day when she was eavesdropping on me and thought I didn't notice, I went on about her and said, "Oh! you got to admit, my lady is one of the loveliest women in the world." All the favors that one little remark conferred on me for a week! I tried on a similar occasion to say that my lady was highly intelligent. Oh! nothing doing, it didn't take; which was just as well, since it was a barefaced lie.

EUPHROSYNE: Sir, I will not stay unless you compel me. I cannot endure any more.

TRIVELIN: That will be enough for now.

CLEANTHIS: I was just going to tell you about the fainting fits my lady is subject to at the slightest smell.

She doesn't know that once, unbeknownst to her, I put flowers on her night-table to see what would come of it. I kept waiting for a fainting fit, it never came. The next day, with company present, she spotted a rose. Bam! Flat on her back.

TRIVELIN: That'll do, Euphrosyne. Go for a walk, a long walk, because I have to have a word with her. She will join you presently.

CLEANTHIS: *(On her way out)* Tell her to be biddable, that's the least she can do. Good-bye, dear friend, I'm glad I've amused you. Some other time I'll tell you how my lady often refrains from wearing fine clothes, but dons a negligé that subtly shows off her figure. That garment is yet another clever snare. Folks assume that a woman who wears such a thing doesn't care about her looks, but don't make me laugh! Stuffing herself into a form-fitting corset, showing off her charms in a nice offhand way. It says: "Take a look at my attractions, they're all mine, they really are"; while on the other hand trying to say: "Look at the way I dress, such simplicity! There's nothing ostentatious about my wardrobe."

TRIVELIN: I asked you to leave us.

CLEANTHIS: I'm going. We'll soon pick up where we left off, and you'll find it most entertaining. Then you'll learn how my lady enters a box at the play, with what timing, what an imposing yet absent-minded, casual air. That brand of arrogance is the product of the very best breeding. You'll see how, once seated in the box, she casts blank and scornful glances at the women on either side and pretends to not to know them. Bye-bye, dear friend, I'm off to our new home. *(She exits.)*

TRIVELIN: This comic sketch has rather annoyed you; but it won't do you any harm.

EUPHROSYNE: You're barbarians.

TRIVELIN: We are civilized people with an educational mission, that's all. There is one more formality you have to perform.

EUPHROSYNE: More formalities!

TRIVELIN: This one is a mere trifle. I have to report what I have just heard and your response to it. Do you admit to all the frivolous conduct, vanity and monkey tricks she just accused you of?

EUPHROSYNE: Admit to them! What! Are such falsehoods credible?

TRIVELIN: Oh! most credible. Be careful. If you admit to them, it will help improve your lot. That's all I'll say... Let's hope that, once you have acknowledged them, someday you may turn your back on all these self-centered follies that divert your kind heart from a wealth of more valuable activities. If, on the other hand, you do not admit to what she said, you will be considered incorrigible, and that will postpone your liberation. Think about it.

EUPHROSYNE: My liberation! Ah! is it possible?

TRIVELIN: Yes, I guarantee it with the aforesaid conditions.

EUPHROSYNE: Soon?

TRIVELIN: Probably.

EUPHROSYNE: Sir, go ahead as if I've admitted to everything.

TRIVELIN: What? You want me to lie?

EUPHROSYNE: After all, these are very peculiar conditions! In fact they're disgusting!

TRIVELIN: A bit humiliating; but that's the point. Make up your mind: a most imminent liberation is the reward of honesty. Come now, don't you resemble the portrait she painted?

EUPHROSYNE: But…

TRIVELIN: What?

EUPHROSYNE: There's some truth in it, give or take.

TRIVELIN: Give or take is beside the point. Do you admit to all the facts? Did she exaggerate? Didn't she tell it like it is? Make haste. I have other things to do.

EUPHROSYNE: Do you need so precise an answer?

TRIVELIN: Yes indeed, madam, and it's all for your own good.

EUPHROSYNE: Well…

TRIVELIN: Go on.

EUPHROSYNE: I am very young…

TRIVELIN: I didn't ask your age.

EUPHROSYNE: A person belongs to a certain class. A person aims to please.

TRIVELIN: And that is what makes the portrait a good likeness.

EUPHROSYNE: I suppose so.

TRIVELIN: Well, that's what we're waiting for. You also find the portrait somewhat amusing, don't you?

EUPHROSYNE: I must confess.

TRIVELIN: Wonderful! I am satisfied, dear lady. Go and join Cleanthis. I am now using her real name as a pledge of my sincerity. Do not lose patience. Be on your best behavior and the hoped-for moment will arrive.

EUPHROSYNE: I trust you.

(EUPHROSYNE *exits.* HARLEQUIN *and* IPHICRATES, *who have changed clothes with one another, enter.*)

HARLEQUIN: Tralala, tralala, tralaloo! Tralaloo! Glad to see you, comrade! The republic's wine is super. I've gone and drunk a full pint of it, for I get so parched now I'm a master I'll soon be thirsting for another pint. Three cheers for the vineyard, the vintner and the wine-cellars of our wonderful republic!

TRIVELIN: Splendid! Enjoy yourself, comrade. Are you pleased with Harlequin?

HARLEQUIN: Yes, he's a fine fellow. I'll make something of 'im yet. Every once in while he gives out a sigh, but I forbade him to do so or suffer corporal punishment for disobeying. I ordered him to be cheerful.

(HARLEQUIN *takes his master by the hand and dances.*)

HARLEQUIN: Tralala la la…

TRIVELIN: Your example makes me cheerful myself.

HARLEQUIN: Oh! whenever the living is easy, it puts me in a good mood.

TRIVELIN: That's fine. I am delighted that you're pleased with Harlequin. I assume he didn't give you much cause for complaint back in his own country?

HARLEQUIN: Huh! Back there? I used to curse him left, right and center. He was impossible to put up with. But right now I'm happy, all is forgiven. We're even.

TRIVELIN: I admire that attitude and find it touching. Does it mean you enjoy your good fortune modestly without trying to give him a hard time?

HARLEQUIN: A hard time! Ah, that pathetic fellow! I may be the tiniest bit abusive, because I'm the master. That's all.

TRIVELIN: Because I am the master. The same old story.

HARLEQUIN: Yes, for when you're the master, you lay down the law, get all high-handed, and a high hand can lead a decent man to go too far at times.

TRIVELIN: Oh! never mind. I can see you're not vindictive.

HARLEQUIN: Goodness no! I'm just playful.

TRIVELIN: *(To* IPHICRATES*)* Don't be alarmed by what I'm about to say. *(To* HARLEQUIN.*)* I need some information. How did he used to behave back there? Was there some flaw in his temper, his character?

HARLEQUIN: *(Laughing)* Ah! comrade, you've got a dirty mind. You want to hear some bad-mouthing.

TRIVELIN: So his was a funny personality?

HARLEQUIN: Word of honor, it was a riot.

TRIVELIN: All right, let's have a laugh.

HARLEQUIN: *(To* IPHICRATES*)* Harlequin, do you promise to laugh too?

IPHICRATES: *(Under his breath)* Do you want to drive me to despair? What are you going to tell him?

HARLEQUIN: Leave it to me. If I offend you, I'll apologize afterwards.

TRIVELIN: It's a mere trifle. It's no more than I asked of the young woman you saw before, concerning her mistress.

HARLEQUIN: I'll bet she gave you an earful of brainless acts and grievances so you'd feel sorry for her, right?

TRIVELIN: True enough.

HARLEQUIN: Well, I can match that. There's not much else to this puppy: a big spender with empty pockets, that's him all over. You want me to hang out dirty linen? Hare-brained by nature, hare-brained from copying bad examples, 'cause that's the way the ladies like 'em. A spendthrift; tight-fisted when he should be open-handed, open-handed when he should be tight-fisted; good at borrowing, bad at paying back.

Ashamed to be well-mannered, proud to be rude. A bit sarcastic about decent people; a bit of a braggart; up to his neck in girl-friends but can't remember their names. That's my boy. Is he worth the trouble of painting a full-length portrait? *(To* IPHICRATES.*)* No, I won't bother, my friend, don't worry.

TRIVELIN: This sketch will suffice. *(To* IPHICRATES.*)* Now we need you to certify and verify what he has just said.

IPHICRATES: Me?

TRIVELIN: You. Just now the lady did the same. She will tell you what made up her mind. Believe me, it will do you more good than you can imagine.

IPHICRATES: Do me good? If that's the case, I might sort of admit to some of it.

HARLEQUIN: Admit it in full. It fits like a glove.

TRIVELIN: I require all or nothing.

IPHICRATES: You would like me to admit I was a laughing-stock?

HARLEQUIN: Who cares since it's in the past?

TRIVELIN: Is that all you have to say?

IPHICRATES: I'll admit to half, just to get out of this mess.

TRIVELIN: All.

IPHICRATES: So be it.

*(*HARLEQUIN *laughs uproariously.)*

TRIVELIN: You have done very well, you'll find it worth your while. Farewell, you'll be hearing from me soon.

*(*TRIVELIN *exits.* CLEANTHIS *and* EUPHROSYNE *enter.)*

CLEANTHIS: Lord Iphicrates, may one inquire what you are laughing at?

HARLEQUIN: I'm laughing at my Harlequin who just admitted he was a laughingstock.

CLEANTHIS: That does surprise me, for he looks like an intelligent fellow. If you'd like to see a self-confessed tease, feast your eyes on my lady's maid.

HARLEQUIN: (Looking at her) I'll be jiggered! With a face as pert as that, she was born to be a servant girl. But let's change the subject, my fair lady. How shall we be amused now that we're free and easy?

CLEANTHIS: Why, by elegant conversation.

HARLEQUIN: I'm afraid that'll make you yawn, I'm yawning already. If I were to make love to you, it'd be much more fun.

CLEANTHIS: Well, do it then. Sigh for me. Try to win my heart, catch it if you can, I won't put up much resistance. But you've got to make an effort. Here I am, waiting with bated breath. But since we are now masters, let's make love in the grand manner. Let's go about it refined, like they do in high society.

HARLEQUIN: All right. Nothing but top o' the line for us.

CLEANTHIS: I've got an idea: we should have those two bring us chairs so we may be comfortably seated as we give ear to the flowery speeches you are about to make. We must keep up appearances, even as we wallow in our pleasures.

HARLEQUIN: Your wish is my command. (To IPHICRATES) Harlequin, quick, a chair for me and a throne for the lady.

IPHICRATES: You expect me to do chores?

HARLEQUIN: The Republic insists.

CLEANTHIS: Never mind, we can promenade just as fashionably. As we converse you will deftly turn the talk to the passion my eyes have ignited in you. But since nowadays we happen to be respectable, mind your Ps & Qs. No back-room horsing around. Come, let us foot it nobly, skimping on neither compliments nor civilities.

HARLEQUIN: And don't you skimp on the pouty faces. Lay it on thick, if only to needle our betters. Should we send away our domestics?

CLEANTHIS: Not at all. What would we do without them? They are our retinue. Just have them keep their distance.

HARLEQUIN: *(To* IPHICRATES*)* Stay ten paces to the rear.

(IPHICRATES *and* EUPHROSYNE *retreat, with gestures of astonishment and dismay.* CLEANTHIS *watches* IPHICRATES *go, and* HARLEQUIN *watches* EUPHROSYNE.*)*

(HARLEQUIN, *strolling along the stage with* CLEANTHIS:*)*

HARLEQUIN: Do you perceive, madam, how bright the sun is shining?

CLEANTHIS: This is the finest climate in the world. It's what they call the loving time of day.

HARLEQUIN: Loving time of day? Then I am like the time, madam.

CLEANTHIS: How so? How are you like it?

HARLEQUIN: Gadzooks! How can a person not be loving when a person finds a person's person smack dab within an inch of a person's charms? *(So saying, he jumps for joy.)* Oh! oh! oh! oh!

CLEANTHIS: What's come over you? You are disfiguring our conversation.

HARLEQUIN: Oh! never mind. I'm just giving myself a hand.

CLEANTHIS: Suppress that hand, it's a distraction. *(Proceeding)* I was well aware that my charms may be at the bottom of this. Sir, you are gallant. You amble along with me, you whisper sweet nothings; but all right already, enough is enough, I dispense with your compliments.

HARLEQUIN: And I thank you in turn for your dispensary.

CLEANTHIS: You are about to proclaim you are in love, I can tell. Speak out, sir, speak. Luckily I won't believe a word of it. You are most attentive, but fickle, and you will not win me over.

HARLEQUIN: *(Stops her in her tracks by taking her arm; getting on his knees)* Must I kneel, madam, to convince you of my passion and the sincerity of my desire?

CLEANTHIS: This is getting serious. Leave off, I don't want any complications. Get up. How impetuous! Do you expect me to say I love you? Can't we leave it at that? What an embarrassing situation.

HARLEQUIN: *(On his knees, laughing)* Ha, ha, ha! This is going well. We're as ridiculous as our bosses, but better behaved.

CLEANTHIS: Oh! If you laugh you spoil it all.

HARLEQUIN: Ha, ha! Honest to goodness, you deserve to be loved and so do I. Do you know what I'm thinking?

CLEANTHIS: What?

HARLEQUIN: First of all, you don't love me, you were just teasing, same as they do in high society.

CLEANTHIS: I don't love you as yet, but I was on the verge when you broke off. And you, do you love me?

HARLEQUIN: I was on the verge too, when something occurred to me. How do you like my Harlequin?

CLEANTHIS: Just my type. And what do you say to my lady's maid?

HARLEQUIN: She's a tasty bit of fluff!

CLEANTHIS: I have an inkling of what's on your mind.

HARLEQUIN: Tell you what: you make love to Harlequin and I'll do the same to your lady's maid. We've got the stuff to make it work.

CLEANTHIS: The very idea tickles me pink. I'm sure they won't be able to resist us.

HARLEQUIN: They've never had a better reason for falling in love. We're perfect matches for them.

CLEANTHIS: It's a deal. Urge Harlequin to take an interest in me. Make him aware of the good it'll do him, given his current situation. If he marries me, he won't be a slave any more. Easy as pie, come to think of it. After all, I used to be a slave, and now at long last I am a great lady and mistress as good as any. It may be down to sheer luck, but isn't luck half the battle in life? What does he say to that? I even have the face of a thoroughbred, so I'm told.

HARLEQUIN: Confound it! I wouldn't mind having you myself, if I didn't love your maid a teensy bit more. Suggest she fall for little old me, who, you can plainly see, is not to be sneezed at.

CLEANTHIS: You'll get your wish. I'm going to call Cleanthis over and have a word with her. Make yourself scarce for a while and then come back. Then you can talk to Harlequin on my behalf, for he has to make the first move. My sex, my modesty and my dignity demand it.

HARLEQUIN: Oh! they may demand it, if that's what you want; but in high society folks aren't so fussy. Skip the foreplay, toss him some blunt little word of encouragement, just at random. After all you're his better in the new order of things.

CLEANTHIS: That's a very good idea. In fact, given my present status, it would be beneath me to go through any empty formalities. I get your drift. But do speak to him, and I shall have a word with Cleanthis. Go back to your quarters for a while.

HARLEQUIN: Play up my good points. Invent some and I'll pay you back in kind.

CLEANTHIS: Leave it to me. *(She calls* EUPHROSYNE.*)* Cleanthis!

*(*HARLEQUIN *and* IPHICRATES *exit.* EUPHROSYNE *comes forward meekly.)*

CLEANTHIS: Come closer and step on it so I don't have to be kept waiting.

EUPHROSYNE: What's the matter?

CLEANTHIS: Come here and pay attention. A highly respectable man has just informed me that he loves you. It's Iphicrates.

EUPHROSYNE: Which one?

CLEANTHIS: Which one? Are there two here? The one who was just with me.

EUPHROSYNE: Ah! What am I supposed to do with his love?

CLEANTHIS: Ah! What were you supposed to do with the love of all those other lovers? Are you brain-dead! Does the word love shock you? You're no stranger to love! Before now the only reason you ever looked at a man was to make him love you. That's all your bright eyes are good for. Do they scorn to seduce Lord Iphicrates? He may not grovel before you. He may not have a silly look on his face and a vapid manner. He may not be a numbskull, some little trifler, a gaudy butterfly, charming but indiscreet. He is none of that. He lacks such attractions, true enough. He's only a simple fellow with simple manners, without the wit to put on airs and graces; he will tell you he loves you simply because it's true. The bottom line is, he's got a good heart, and that's that; and I'm sorry he's not more exciting. But you're no fool. I've decided he's your intended, he will improve your standing here, and you will be good enough to entertain his love and be sensible, you hear? You will carry out my intentions, I expect. Never forget this is what I want.

EUPHROSYNE: Where am I? What next? *(She is lost in thought.)*

(Enter HARLEQUIN *who bows to* CLEANTHIS, *as she exits. He goes over and tugs* EUPHROSYNE *by the sleeve.)*

EUPHROSYNE: What do you want of me?

HARLEQUIN: Heh, heh, heh! Has anyone said anything about me?

EUPHROSYNE: Please let go of me.

HARLEQUIN: Ah! now, now, look me in the eye and guess what I'm thinking.

EUPHROSYNE: Think whatever you like.

HARLEQUIN: Can't you figure out what I'm trying to say?

EUPHROSYNE: No.

HARLEQUIN: That's because I haven't said anything yet.

EUPHROSYNE: *(Impatient)* Oh really!

HARLEQUIN: Don't pretend. You've been told what's in my heart. You're one lucky girl.

EUPHROSYNE: What a situation!

HARLEQUIN: You think I'm a bit of a booby, right? But you'll get over it. The fact is I love you and I don't know how to put it into words.

EUPHROSYNE: You?

HARLEQUIN: Yes, blast it! What else can a man do? You're so beautiful! A man just has to fling his heart at your feet; all you've got to do is pick it up.

EUPHROSYNE: Can I sink any lower?

HARLEQUIN: *(Looking at her hands)* What bewitching hands! What dainty little fingers! How happy they would make me! This heart of mine would tingle at their touch. My Queen, my heart's made of putty, but it doesn't show. If you were gracious enough to be putty-hearted too, oh! I'd go crazy on the spot.

EUPHROSYNE: You're crazy enough as it is.

HARLEQUIN: I could never be as crazy as you deserve.

EUPHROSYNE: All I deserve is pity, my friend.

HARLEQUIN: Right, right! You're telling me? You deserve all the desserts imaginable. An emperor isn't in your league, and neither am I. But here I am, in the flesh, and an emperor isn't; and a nobody on the spot is worth a somebody who isn't. What do you say?

EUPHROSYNE: Harlequin, I don't think you're a bad person.

HARLEQUIN: Oh! I'm not like I was before. I'm sheepish as a…sheep.

EUPHROSYNE: Then respect my distressing situation.

HARLEQUIN: You bet! I kneel down before it.

EUPHROSYNE: Do not persecute an unhappy woman, just because you can do so with impunity. Behold the pitiful status to which I am reduced; and if you don't care about the position I once held in society,

my birth, my breeding, at least let my disgrace, my
enslavement, my grief melt your heart. Here you can
abuse me as much as you please, I have no refuge and
no defender, only my despair to speak in my defense. I
need other people to commiserate with me, even you,
Harlequin. That's how low I've sunk. Don't you think
I'm miserable enough? You've been set free so you're
happy. Why should that make you wicked? I'm too
forlorn to say any more. I've never done you harm. Do
not add to what I already suffer. *(She exits.)*

HARLEQUIN: *(Crushed, his arms dangling; he doesn't make
a move)* I'm speechless.

(Enter IPHICRATES.*)*

IPHICRATES: Cleanthis said you had something to tell
me. What is it? Thought up some new insults?

HARLEQUIN: Somebody else who wants me to feel
sorry for them. I've nothing to say to you, my friend,
except I wish you'd follow orders and love the new
Euphrosyne. That's all. What's the hell is wrong with
you?

IPHICRATES: Can you ask such a thing of me,
Harlequin?

HARLEQUIN: Huh! Yes, I damn well can, since I just did.

IPHICRATES: I've been promised that my enslavement
will end soon, but it's a trick. This is the end, I give up,
I am dying, Harlequin, and soon you will be free of this
wretched master who never thought you capable of the
abuse he's suffered at your hands.

HARLEQUIN: Ha! That's all right then, and now we can
kiss and make up. Listen, I forbid you to die out of
spite. Disease, fine, go right ahead.

IPHICRATES: The gods will punish you, Harlequin.

HARLEQUIN: Hey! What for? For being downtrodden my whole life?

IPHICRATES: For your impudence and your contempt for your master. I've never felt so humiliated, I confess. You were born and raised with me in my father's house. Your father is still on the estate. He instructed you in your duty when you left home. I personally chose you out of a feeling of friendship to accompany me on my travels. I thought you cared for me, and that made me fond of you.

HARLEQUIN: *(Weeping)* Eh! Who said I don't care for you?

IPHICRATES: You care for me, and yet you pepper me with insults?

HARLEQUIN: Because I'm teasing you a teeny-weeny bit. Does that mean I don't care for you? You say you're fond of me, all the time you were having me beaten. Is thrashing a more genuine sign of affection than teasing?

IPHICRATES: I admit I may have ill-used you at times for no good reason.

HARLEQUIN: That's the honest truth.

IPHICRATES: But didn't I make up for it with plenty of kindnesses?

HARLEQUIN: Not to my knowledge.

IPHICRATES: Besides, didn't I have to correct your faults?

HARLEQUIN: I suffered more from yours than mine. My greatest faults were your ill temper, your bossiness, and the neglect of your poor slave.

IPHICRATES: Go on, you're nothing but an ingrate. You should be helping me here, sharing my affliction, setting your comrades an example by a devotion so

moving it might perhaps persuade them to put aside
their custom or set me free. And I would be eternally
grateful to you!

HARLEQUIN: You're right, my friend. You point out
what my duty to you should be in this place; but you
never did your duty to me when we were in Athens.
You want me to share your affliction, but you never
shared mine. Well, all right, my feelings ought to be
more tender than yours; for I've been suffering a longer
time and I know what hardship means. You beat me
'cause you were fond of me. Since you say so, I forgive
you. I teased you just for fun, take it in the right spirit,
and learn by it. I'll speak to my comrades on your
behalf, I'll plead with them to send you away and, if
they won't, I'll keep you as my friend; for I am not like
you. I wouldn't have the heart to be happy at your
expense.

IPHICRATES: *(Drawing near* HARLEQUIN*)* My dear
Harlequin, after what I've just heard, heaven grant
that one day I have the pleasure of returning the favor!
Go, my dear boy, forget you were my slave and I shall
always remember I did not deserve to be your master.

HARLEQUIN: Don't talk like that, dear boss. If I had
been your equal, maybe I would have been as bad
as you. I should be begging your forgiveness for the
awful servant I always was. Whenever you went off
the deep end, it was my fault.

IPHICRATES: *(Embracing him)* Your generosity
overwhelms me.

HARLEQUIN: My poor boss, doesn't it feel nice to do
good!

(HARLEQUIN *begins to undress his master.*)

IPHICRATES: What are you doing, my friend?

HARLEQUIN: Give me back my clothes, and put on your own. I'm not worthy to wear them.

IPHICRATES: I can't keep down the tears. Do what you will.

(Enter CLEANTHIS *and* EUPHROSYNE *who is weeping.)*

CLEANTHIS: Leave me, I've got better things to do than listen to you snivel. *(And closer to* HARLEQUIN*)* What's the meaning of this, Lord Iphicrates? Why have you put on your old clothes?

HARLEQUIN: *(Tenderly)* They were too tight on my dear friend, and his were too baggy on me.

*(*HARLEQUIN *embraces his master's knees.)*

CLEANTHIS: Then explain this sight. Can you be begging his pardon?

HARLEQUIN: As punishment for my insolence.

CLEANTHIS: But what about our project?

HARLEQUIN: Turns out I want to do the right thing. Isn't that a lovely project? I repent my stupidity, he repents his. Repent yours, Madam Euphrosyne will repent hers; and then three cheers for us! It'll add up to four fine repentances and make us cry to our heart's content.

EUPHROSYNE: Ah! my dear Cleanthis, what an example for you!

IPHICRATES: Say rather: what an example for us all! Madam, you see me won over.

CLEANTHIS: Is that so! What fine examples you've set for us, I must say. Here are these two who despised us back home, acted high and mighty, mistreated us, and looked down on us as earthworms; and now they're overjoyed to find we're a hundred times more decent than they ever were. Fie! How vile to have had nothing but gold, silver and a position in society to your credit!

Nothing to be proud of there! Where would you be today if we had thought you were no better than that? Come, come, wouldn't you be in a fine pickle? When it comes to forgiving you, what does a person have to be to act so generously, may I ask? Rich? No. Aristocratic? No. Lord of the manor? Certainly not. You were all that. Does that make you worth anything? Then what does it take? Ah! there's the rub. You have to have a kind heart, virtue and intelligence. That's what matters, that's what counts, that's what raises us up, what makes one person better than another. Do you hear, my upstanding members of high society? That's what creates the good examples you insist on having but never on being. And who do you ask it of? The poor people you have always offended, abused, oppressed, rich as you are, and who today take pity on you, poor as they are. Puff yourselves up with pride now, make a show of your arrogance, you will be forgiven! Get out, you ought to blush for shame.

HARLEQUIN: Come, come, my friend, let's be better than that and no recriminations. Let's do the right thing without insults. They're sorry for their bad actions, which means they're our equals, for when a person is sorry, he's good; and when a person is good, he's as far up the ladder as we are. Come closer, Lady Euphrosyne. She forgives you. Look at her weep. Put an end to resentment, the matter is settled.

CLEANTHIS: He's right, I'm weeping. You can't say I don't have a tender heart.

EUPHROSYNE: (Sadly) My dear Cleanthis, I abused the authority I had over you, I admit it.

CLEANTHIS: Honest to goodness! How did you have the gall to act that way? But what's done is done, I'm willing to forget it. Do as you please. If you made me suffer, that's on your head. I don't want to have to blame myself for the same thing. I set you free. And if a ship were on hand, I would leave with you at once. That's all the harm I wish you. If you ever harm me again, though, it won't be my fault.

HARLEQUIN: *(Weeping)* Ah! what a good girl! Ah! what a generous nature!

IPHICRATES: Are you satisfied, madam?

EUPHROSYNE: *(Melting)* Let me embrace you, my dear Cleanthis.

HARLEQUIN: *(To* CLEANTHIS*)* Get down on your knees if you want to one-up her.

EUPHROSYNE: Gratitude barely leaves me strength to respond. Stop talking about your past enslavement, and from now on think only to share all the blessings the gods have lavished on me, if we ever get back to Athens.

*(*TRIVELIN *enters.)*

TRIVELIN: What do I see? You're weeping, my children. You're embracing?

HARLEQUIN: Ah! That's only the obvious bit. We are paragons of virtue. We are kings and queens. It's all over, peace is declared, virtue is triumphant. What we need now is a boat and a boatman to take us home; and if you let us have them, you will be almost as decent people as us.

TRIVELIN: What about you, Cleanthis, do you share his sentiments?

CLEANTHIS: *(Kissing her mistress's hand)* Need I say more? You see how things stand.

HARLEQUIN: *(Also taking his master's hand to kiss it)* That's my last word too. This action speaks louder than a thousand words.

TRIVELIN: I am delighted. Embrace me as well, my dear children. This is what I've been waiting for. If it hadn't come about, we would have punished your revenge, as we had punished their harshness. And you, Iphicrates, and you, Euphrosyne, I see you are moved. I have nothing to add to the lessons this episode has taught you. You were their masters and you behaved badly. They became your masters and they forgave you. Give some thought to that. Differences in rank and station are only a test the gods impose on us. I'll leave it at that. You shall depart in two days' time and see Athens again. May present joy and gladness make up for the suffering you've undergone. Now celebrate the most meaningful day you ever lived.

END OF PLAY

THE COLONY
(*LA COLONIE*—1750)

CHARACTERS & SETTING

ARTHENICE, *a noblewoman*
MRS SORBIN, *a tradesman's wife*
MR SORBIN, *her husband*
TIMAGENES, *a nobleman*
LINA, MRS SORBIN's daughter
PERSINET, *a young commoner,* LINA's *boy-friend*
HERMOCRATES, *a notary, taken to be a noble*
Group of women, both nobles and commoners

The scene is an island to which all the characters have migrated.

(Enter ARTHENICE *and* MRS SORBIN.*)*

ARTHENICE: Well now! Mrs Sorbin, or should I say colleague. That's what you are, now that the women of your class have elected you to the same office conferred on me by the noblewomen. Let us shake hands, join forces and be of one mind.

MRS SORBIN: *(Giving her her hand)* Resolved: we two make up one woman with one idea.

ARTHENICE: Now we are charged with the greatest mission our sex has ever had. And it comes at a most opportune moment for affirming our rights relative to men.

MRS SORBIN: Oh! but this time, gentlemen, we shall arrange matters in partnership.

ARTHENICE: Ever since we had to take refuge on this island with them, we've been stuck here with no central government.

MRS SORBIN: Yes, we need a brand-new order, the time has come. This is where we can demand justice and cast off the absurd servility that's been imposed on us ever since the dawn of human existence. We'd rather die than put up with such humiliation any longer.

ARTHENICE: Good for you. Do you sincerely feel you have the courage equal to the magnitude of your task?

MRS SORBIN: Why, today I care not a fig for life. Long story short, I'm all for self-sacrifice. I shall devote my whole being to the cause. Mrs Sorbin is more eager to live in history than in society.

ARTHENICE: I promise you your name will be immortal.

MRS SORBIN: In twenty thousand years, we will still be the news of the day.

ARTHENICE: And even if we do not succeed, our granddaughters will.

MRS SORBIN: I tell you the men will never see it coming. Incidentally, it's all very well to question my sincerity, but there's a certain Lord Timagenes round here who's been laying siege to your heart. Is he still at it? Is the siege over? That would be a terrible example of female frailty, be on your guard against it.

ARTHENICE: Who is this Timagenes, Mrs Sorbin? I have broken off relations with him ever since we undertook our project. Be steadfast and think only of following my example

MRS SORBIN: Who? Me? Where's the problem? All I've got is a husband, what does it cost me to leave him? Love's got nothing to do with it.

ARTHENICE: Oh, I agree!

MRS SORBIN: Well now! you're aware that at any moment the men are going to gather in the tents, to choose two of their number to make our laws. The drum roll is to summon the assembly.

ARTHENICE: What of it?

MRS SORBIN: What of it? What we have to do is beat our own drum. It will enjoin our women to reject those gentlemen's rules and regulations. On the spot we'll draw up a neat and tidy act of separation from the men, who so far haven't a clue.

ARTHENICE: Just what I was thinking, but instead of a drum roll, I would like to post the proclamation to the blare of a trumpet.

MRS SORBIN: Right, a trumpet's a great idea, just the ticket.

ARTHENICE: There go Timagenes and your husband passing us by without a look in our direction.

MRS SORBIN: I guess they're on their way to the Council meeting. Do you think we should call them over?

ARTHENICE: All right, let's question them about what's going on. *(She calls to* TIMAGENES.*)*

MRS SORBIN: *(Also calls)* Yoohoo! Husband o'mine!

(Enter MR SORBIN *and* TIMAGENES.*)*

TIMAGENES: Ah! forgive me, fair Arthenice, I did not think you were so near.

MR SORBIN: What do you want, wife? We're in a hurry.

MRS SORBIN: Tut, tut, take it easy. I want to see you, Mr Sorbin, to say good morning. Do you have anything to say to me, trivial or otherwise?

MR SORBIN: No, what I am supposed to say, except what the weather's like or the time of day?

ARTHENICE: And you, Timagenes, what have you to inform me? Is there talk of the women amongst you?

TIMAGENES: No, madam, I know nothing concerning them. No one has said a word on the subject.

ARTHENICE: Not a word, a fine state of affairs.

MRS SORBIN: Patience, the proclamation will light a fire under them.

MR SORBIN: What proclamation is that?

MRS SORBIN: Oh! nothing, I'm just talking.

ARTHENICE: Ah! Tell me, Timagenes, where are you both off to with such solemn faces?

TIMAGENES: We've been summoned to the Council meeting, where the aristocracy and nobility on one hand and the commoners on the other plan to appoint us, this honest man and myself, to draft the laws. I admit my incompetence is already making me nervous.

MRS SORBIN: What, husband, you're going to make laws?

MR SORBIN: Sorry to say, it's been decreed, and it's one big headache.

MRS SORBIN: Why so, Mr Sorbin? Even though you're a dunce and a bit thick, I've always known you to have very good horse-sense. That should come in handy in this matter. Besides, I'm sure those gentlemen will be clear-headed enough to ask the women to assist them, as is only reasonable.

MR SORBIN: Ah! stop harping on your women, it's no laughing matter!

MRS SORBIN: Well, I for one am not laughing.

MR SORBIN: Have you gone crazy?

MRS SORBIN: Goodness me, Mr Sorbin, for someone who represents the commoners you are very rude; but luckily there will be a statute dealing with that. I can lay down the law too.

MR SORBIN: (Laughs) You! Ha, ha, ha, ha!

TIMAGENES: (Laughing) Ha, ha, ha, ha!

ARTHENICE: What's so funny about that? She's right, she will, and so will I.

TIMAGENES: You, madam?

MR SORBIN: (Laughing) Laws!

ARTHENICE: Definitely.

MR SORBIN: (Laughing) Well, go ahead, please yourselves, have your fun, play the fool; but save your clowning for some other time. Your jokes're out of keeping at the moment.

TIMAGENES: Why? High spirits are always in season.

ARTHENICE: High spirits, Timagenes?

MRS SORBIN: Our clowning, Mr Sorbin? Watch out, we'll show you clowning.

MR SORBIN: Let's leave these jokers, Lord Timagenes, and be on our way. Good-bye, wife, you've been lots of help.

ARTHENICE: Wait, I have a couple of comments to make to the gentleman elected by the nobility.

TIMAGENES: Speak, madam.

ARTHENICE: Your attention, please. We have been obliged, great and small, nobility, middle-class and commoners, to abandon our homeland to avoid death or enslavement at the hands of the enemy who defeated us.

MR SORBIN: This sounds to me like a history lesson. Let's postpone it till we've got some free time, we're too busy right now.

MRS SORBIN: Quiet, you ill-mannered creature.

TIMAGENES: We are listening.

ARTHENICE: Our ships brought us to this uncivilized land, but the land is a good one.

MR SORBIN: Trouble is, our women never shut up.

MRS SORBIN: *(Angrily)* Again!

ARTHENICE: The plan was to settle here, but since we disembarked higgledy-piggledy, and fate made us all equal and no one has the right to command and everything is in a state of confusion, we need leaders, we need one person in charge or many, we need laws.

TIMAGENES: And that's just what we're going to provide, madam.

MR SORBIN: We'll have all that right away, they're waiting for us to put the plan into action.

ARTHENICE: Who's us? Who do you mean by us?

MR SORBIN: For goodness' sake, we mean us, who else can there be?

ARTHENICE: Not so fast. These laws, just who is going to make them, who is to enact them?

MR SORBIN: *(Mocking)* Us.

MRS SORBIN: Men!

MR SORBIN: Obviously.

ARTHENICE: These leaders, or that leader, will be chosen from among whom?

MRS SORBIN: *(Sarcastic)* Men.

MR SORBIN: Well, obviously!

ARTHENICE: Who will the leader be?

MRS SORBIN: A man.

MR SORBIN: Who else?

ARTHENICE: Always men and never women, what do you think of that, Timagenes? Since your fellow legislator's dim wits can't figure out what I'm driving at.

TIMAGENES: I confess, madam, that I don't see the difficulty either.

ARTHENICE: You don't see it? That'll do, you may go.

MR SORBIN: *(To his wife)* Tell us what this is all about.

MRS SORBIN: If you have to ask, you might as well get out.

TIMAGENES: But, madam…

ARTHENICE: But, sir, you are annoying me.

MR SORBIN: *(To his wife)* What does she mean?

MRS SORBIN: Go take your man's face somewhere else.

MR SORBIN: What's got their goat?

MRS SORBIN: Always men, never women, and that means nothing to you.

MR SORBIN: What of it?

MRS SORBIN: Hum! You're a nincompoop, that's what of it.

TIMAGENES: You distress me, madam, if you insist I go without letting me know why I have fallen into disfavor.

ARTHENICE: On your way, sir, you'll find out when you return from your Council meeting.

MRS SORBIN: The drum will tell you the rest or else a proclamation to the blare of the trumpet.

MR SORBIN: Fife, trumpet or bugle, I could care less. Let's go, Lord Timagenes.

TIMAGENES: Now that you're caused me anxiety, madam, I shall return as soon as possible.

(MR SORBIN *and* TIMAGENES *exit.*)

ARTHENICE: Inability to understand us is grounds for fresh outrage.

MRS SORBIN: The age-old custom of snubbing us is passed down from father to son, and clogs their brains.

(*Enter* LINA *and* PERSINET.)

PERSINET: Here I am, esteemed mother-in-law-to-be. You promised me the charming Lina; and I can't wait to be her husband. I love her so much that love without marriage is past enduring.

ARTHENICE: (*To* MRS SORBIN) Get rid of this young man, Mrs Sorbin. Current events require us to cut off relations with all his species.

MRS SORBIN: You're right, such relations are no longer fitting.

PERSINET: I'm waiting for an answer.

MRS SORBIN: What are you doing here, Persinet?

PERSINET: For heaven's sake! I'm pleading with you and I'm escorting my peerless Lina.

MRS SORBIN: Go back where you came from.

LINA: Go back where he came from! Hey! What brought that on?

MRS SORBIN: I want him to be gone, he'd better, present circumstances demand it, it's a matter of government policy.

LINA: He could walk behind us at a distance.

PERSINET: Yes, I'll be happy to trail humbly in the rear.

MRS SORBIN: No, that won't do, I won't have it. Be off with you, don't come near us until peace is declared.

LINA: Till we meet again, Persinet, see you soon. Let's not antagonize my mother.

PERSINET: But who broke the peace? Confounded war, till you're over I'll have to eat my heart out all on my lonesome. (He exits.)

LINA: Why are you so mean to him, mother? Don't you want him to love me any more or marry me?

MRS SORBIN: No, daughter, at the present time love is mere foolishness.

LINA: Dear oh dear! What a pity!

ARTHENICE: And marriage, such as it has been so far, is no more than utter slavery and we abolish it, sweet child. But, to put her mind at ease, we must school her.

LINA: Abolish marriage! Oh! What will you put in its place?

MRS SORBIN: Nothing.

LINA: That's pretty harsh.

ARTHENICE: You know, Lina, that up to now women have always been subservient to their husbands.

LINA: Yes, madam, but that tradition doesn't get in the way of love.

MRS SORBIN: I forbid you love.

LINA: If love exists, how are you going to get rid of it? I didn't go out and catch it; it caught me, and anyway I don't mind being subservient.

MRS SORBIN: How dare you say subservient, you petty slavish soul, honest to goodness! Subservient, on a woman's lips! Before I hear you utter such a horror again, learn that we are fomenting a rebellion.

ARTHENICE: Don't get carried away, she isn't privy to our plans yet because she is still a minor, but I'll answer for her once she's put in the picture. I'm sure she will be delighted to have as much authority as her husband over her little household, and whenever he says: I want, to be able to reply: well, I don't.

LINA: *(Weeping)* I won't need to bother. Persinet and I, we always want the same thing; we're well matched.

MRS SORBIN: Mind what you're about with your Persinet. If your ambitions aren't any higher than that, I'll drum you out of the corps of women. Stick with my colleague and me and learn to realize your importance; and do dry those tears which distress your mother and diminish our dignity.

ARTHENICE: I see some of our friends coming. They seem eager to tell us something, let's see what they want.

(Enter four WOMEN, *two of whom carry a striped ribbon bracelet.)*

ONE OF THE DEPUTIES: Esteemed comrades, the sex which appointed you its leaders and chose you to defend it has by a recent resolution deemed it proper to bestow upon you tokens of your worthiness. We bring them on its behalf. We are also charged to swear to you our complete obedience, once you have sworn, your hands in ours, inviolate loyalty: two essential articles which were overlooked before.

ARTHENICE: Illustrious deputies, we would gladly dispense with the adornments with which you array us. It would have sufficed to be adorned with our virtues; it is by those tokens that we must be recognized.

MRS SORBIN: Never mind, let's take 'em anyway. Two bangles are better than one.

ARTHENICE: Nevertheless we accept the honors you heap on us, and we shall tender our oaths, whose omission has been most judiciously noted. Let me begin.

(ARTHENICE *puts her hand in that of one of the* DEPUTIES.)

ARTHENICE: I swear to live to uphold the rights of my downtrodden sex. I consecrate my life to its glory. I swear by my dignity as a woman, by my heart's unbending pride, which is heaven-sent, make no mistake; finally by my inflexible will which was always on hand during my marriage and which saved me from the affront of obeying my late brute of a husband, I have spoken. You're up next, Mrs Sorbin.

MRS SORBIN: Come closer, daughter, hear me and be forever famous, if only for having been present on such a memorable occasion.

(MRS SORBIN *puts her hand in that of one of the* DEPUTIES.)

Hear my words: You shall be on a par with men; they shall be your comrades and not your masters.

Everywhere Mrs will be equal to Mr, or I shall die trying. I swear by the greatest oath I know; by this brow of iron which will never bend and which no one so far can claim to have humbled, just ask around.

ONE OF THE DEPUTIES: Hearken now to what all the women we represent swear to you in turn. The world may end, the human race die out before we fail to obey your orders. Here comes one of our comrades already, hurrying to pay her respects.

(Enter a WOMAN.*)*

WOMAN: I hasten to do homage to our rulers and count myself subject to their laws.

ARTHENICE: Let us embrace, my friends; our mutual oath has just imposed heavy duties on us. To encourage you to perform yours, I feel I must now paint a lurid picture of the degradation we have suffered previously. If I do so, I am only following the example of all party leaders.

MRS SORBIN: It's called stirring up one's base before the battle.

ARTHENICE: But decorum requires that we be seated, we can talk more comfortably.

MRS SORBIN: There are benches over there, we have only to bring them over. *(To* LINA*)* Go to it, little girl, up and at'em.

LINA: I see Persinet passing by. He's stronger than me, and he can help, if you let him.

ONE OF THE WOMEN: What! Make use of a man?

ARTHENICE: Why not? Let the man serve us, I accept it as a good omen.

MRS SORBIN: Well said; in this case it'll bring us luck. *(To* LINA*)* Call the flunkey over.

LINA: *(Calls)* Persinet! Persinet!

(PERSINET *runs in.*)

PERSINET: What's the matter, my love?

LINA: Help me push these benches over here.

PERSINET: With pleasure, but don't you touch them, your little hands are far too dainty, let me do it.

(PERSINET *brings the benches forward.* ARTHENICE *and* MRS SORBIN, *after some civilities, are the first to sit;* PERSINET *and* LINA *both sit at the end of the same bench.*)

ARTHENICE: *(To* PERSINET*)* I wonder at the liberty you take, little boy. Remove yourself, your presence is no longer required.

MRS SORBIN: Your work is done, so skedaddle.

LINA: He takes up almost no space, mother, only half of mine.

MRS SORBIN: Away with you, you hear me.

PERSINET: This is awfully hard to take! *(He exits.)*

ARTHENICE: *(After having coughed and spit)* The tyranny we live under, imposed by our oppressors, makes no sense despite its antiquity. Let us not expect men will turn over a new leaf. Their laws are too inadequate to punish them for making such laws to suit themselves; and unless we intervene, nothing will compel them to do us proper justice. They are not even aware that they are depriving us of it.

MRS SORBIN: That's the way of the world, it's plain to see.

ARTHENICE: As things stand now, the consensus has always been that women have no common sense. So it's taken for granted and we don't even complain.

ONE OF THE WOMEN: Ha! What do you expect! They shout as us from the day we're born: You're incompetent, don't get involved, you're good for nothing but being ladylike. They fed it to our mothers who believed it and repeated it to us. This misinformation was dinned into our ears; so we're docile, inertia takes over, we can be led like sheep.

MRS SORBIN: Oh! I may be only a woman, but as soon as I reached the age of reason, this sheep jumped the fence.

ARTHENICE: I may be only a woman, says Mrs Sorbin, I can't believe it!

MRS SORBIN: That's what comes of sheepishness.

ARTHENICE: We must really have a most laudable distrust of our own intelligence to utter such an uncouth phrase. Find me men who would say the same about themselves. It can't be done. Still, let's see if it's true: you may be only a woman, you say? Ha! What finer thing would you want to be?

MRS SORBIN: Oh! I'll stay as I am, ladies, I'll stay as I am, we do have it better, and I thank heaven for making me one, it has lavished honors upon me, my gratitude is unbounded.

ONE OF THE WOMEN: Bless my soul! You couldn't say fairer than that.

ARTHENICE: Then we should be sure of our worth, not out of pride, but out of gratitude.

LINA: Ah! if you could hear Persinet on the subject, he's absolutely sure of our merits.

ONE OF THE WOMEN: Persinet is persona non grata. It's indecent to mention him.

MRS SORBIN: Hush, little girl, hold your tongue and prick up your ears. Excuse her, ladies; go on, comrade.

ARTHENICE: Let us analyze what we are, and stop me if I go too far. What is a woman, judging merely by outward appearance? Truly, wouldn't you say the gods have made her the object of their most loving attentions?

ONE OF THE WOMEN: The more I think about it, the more I'm convinced.

ONE OF THE WOMEN: It's undeniable.

ANOTHER WOMAN: Totally undeniable.

ANOTHER WOMAN: It's a fact.

ARTHENICE: Looking at her is a treat for the eyes.

A WOMAN: You might say a sheer delight.

ARTHENICE: Allow me to finish.

A WOMAN: No more interruptions.

ANOTHER WOMAN: Yes, we're all ears.

ANOTHER WOMAN: Quiet, please.

ANOTHER WOMAN: Our leader is speaking.

ANOTHER WOMAN: And speaking very well.

LINA: I won't say a word.

MRS SORBIN: Will you all be still? You're getting on my nerves!

ARTHENICE: Let me start over: looking at her is a treat for the eyes. Grace and beauty, in all their forms, compete as to which will endow her face and figure with greater charms.. Ah! Who can possibly describe the number and variety of those charms? Our senses can appreciate them, but our means of expression are too poor to describe them.

(All the WOMEN *sit up straight at this.* ARTHENICE *goes on.)*

ARTHENICE: Woman has a noble presence and yet her air of modesty is enchanting.

(Here the WOMEN *assume an air of modesty.)*

A WOMAN: That's us all right.

MRS SORBIN: Hush!

ARTHENICE: It is a proud beauty, and yet a delicate one; it inspires a respect none dare challenge, unless she permits it. It awakes a love that cannot go unspoken. To say she is beautiful, that she is loveable, is only to begin to sketch her likeness. To say that her beauty takes your breath away, that it overpowers, gladdens, ravishes is almost to say that one's eyes merely skim the surface of one's imagination.

MRS SORBIN: And what's most incredible is that she lives with all those wonders as if they didn't exist. That's really amazing, but I didn't mean to interrupt, not a peep!

ARTHENICE: Let us turn to intelligence and see how alarming ours must have seemed to our tyrants. Judge by the precautions they have taken to stifle it, to prevent us from using it. Spinning, weaving, keeping household accounts, the tedious drudgery of running their homes, ultimately frittering away our time, that's what these gentlemen have condemned us to.

A WOMAN: Honestly, it cries out for vengeance.

ARTHENICE: Or else, we're supposed to shop for clothes, entertain them at their dinner-parties, arouse pleasant passions in them, reign over trifles, our persons being the most trifling trifles of them all. Those are the only functions they leave us here on earth; we who have civilized them, taught them manners, tempered the ferocity of their natures; we, without whom the earth would be but a dwelling for savages unworthy of the name of human beings.

ONE OF THE WOMEN: Ah! the ingrates. Come on, ladies: from this day forth no more dinner-parties.

ANOTHER WOMAN: And as for passions, they can whistle for 'em.

MRS SORBIN: Long story short, let them do the spinning for a change.

ARTHENICE: It is true that they regard us as charming creatures, heavenly bodies, compare our complexions to lilies and roses, extol us in verse, in which the offended sun pales in shame when we appear, and, as you can see, that is no little thing; and then the raptures, the ecstasies, the despairs they treat us to, whenever we let them.

MRS SORBIN: Honestly, it's like pacifying a baby with candy.

ANOTHER WOMAN: Candy, that we've been living off of for six thousand years.

ARTHENICE: What's the result? In our simplicity we cling to the vile honor of pleasing them, and we well and truly enjoy being teases, which we are, you must agree.

A WOMAN: Is that our fault? That's all we're allowed to do.

ARTHENICE: No doubt; but what is remarkable is that the superiority of our soul is so invincible, so obstinate, that it resists everything I've just described, it bursts forth and pierces through the degraded state we have fallen into. We are teases, I admit, but our very teasing is something magnificent.

A WOMAN: Oh! whatever comes out of us is perfect.

ARTHENICE: When I think of all the genius, all the wisdom, all the intelligence that every one of us puts into our self-deception, the only place we can put it, I'm overwhelmed. More strength of mind goes into that than is needed to govern two worlds like this one, and all that brain-power is wasted by it.

MRS SORBIN: *(Angrily)* It's a total loss. It makes you want to cry.

ARTHENICE: All our intelligence ends up muddling their tiny minds so that they don't know what to do with it. It only earns us the silly compliments that their vices and their dim wits, not their reason, lavish on us. Their rational mind has never done anything but insult us.

MRS SORBIN: Come now, no half-measures: I vow to be ugly, and our first edict will be that we all should try to look ugly. *(To* ARTHENICE*)* Am I right, comrade?

ARTHENICE: I agree.

ONE OF THE WOMEN: Look ugly? Seems to me that's the wrong tack to take.

ANOTHER WOMAN: I'll never go along with that either.

ANOTHER WOMAN: Hey! Who could? What! Make ourselves ugly so as to take revenge on men? Hey! Just the opposite, let's make ourselves more glamorous, if that's possible, so they'll miss us that much more.

ANOTHER WOMAN: Yes, so they'll sigh more than ever at our feet, and die of a broken heart when they find they're rebuffed. That's what I call a common-sense payback. You're in the wrong, Mrs Sorbin, completely in the wrong.

MRS SORBIN: Ya-ta-ya-ta-ya-ta. What I say is, if we count on glamor we'll fall back in retreat. Twenty gallants dying at our feet, yet all but one survives. In fact they usually all survive. Those dying men get away with murder. I know our natures only too well, so our edict will stand: we shall make ourselves ugly. Anyway it won't be such a great loss, ladies, and you will lose more by it than I.

A WOMAN: Oh! Not so fast, it's easy for you to say, you haven't much at stake. You're halfway down that road already.

A WOMAN: It's no surprise you hold your attractions so cheap.

A WOMAN: No one would ever take you for a heavenly body.

LINA: Goodness, nor you for a star.

A WOMAN: Cut your cackle, you little feather-brain.

MRS SORBIN: Ah! is that so? You astound me. Hey! Tell me, you puffed-up ninnies, do you think you're good-looking?

ANOTHER WOMAN: Huh! But if we look like you, why do we need to make ourselves ugly? Where do we start?

ANOTHER WOMAN: It's true, it's easy for the Sorbin woman to talk.

MRS SORBIN: What do you mean, the Sorbin woman? Call me the Sorbin woman?

LINA: My mother a Sorbin woman!

MRS SORBIN: Who do you think is in charge here, disrespecting me this way?

ARTHENICE: *(To the other* WOMAN*)* You are out of order, my good woman, and I consider Mrs Sorbin's scheme to be very well-considered.

A WOMAN: Ah, I can believe it. You've got no more at stake than she has.

ARTHENICE: What's that supposed to mean? An attack on my person?

MRS SORBIN: Just look at these baboons with their idea of beauty. Yes, Lady Arthenice and I are your betters. We wish, order and insist that you dress like scarecrows, wear your bonnets back to front, and sun-tan your faces.

ARTHENICE: And to satisfy these women present our edict will make an exception for them alone. They will be permitted to beautify themselves, if they can.

MRS SORBIN: Ah! Well said. Yes, keep all your frills, corsets, ribbons, with your simpering and your laughable affectations, your little pumps or slippers that won't fit without squeezing your massive hoof in them, trying to make it dainty, primp and preen, primp and preen, it won't make an ounce of difference.

ONE OF THE WOMEN: Honest to goodness! How rude! What were we thinking when we chose her?

ARTHENICE: Withdraw. Your oaths bind you, obey. The meeting is adjourned.

ONE OF THE WOMEN: Obey? Such airs and graces.

ONE OF THE WOMEN: We must make a complaint, lodge a formal protest.

ALL THE WOMEN. Yes, we protest, we protest, we object.

MRS SORBIN: I admit, my fists are itching for a fight.

ARTHENICE: Withdraw, I tell you, or I shall put you under arrest.

ONE OF THE WOMEN: *(Leaving with the others)* It's your own fault, ladies, I didn't want anything to do with that market woman or that stuck-up princess, I wanted no part of it, but nobody listened to me.

(Exit the WOMEN.*)*

LINA: Oh dear! Mother, for the sake of peace, let us keep our pumps and our corsets.

MRS SORBIN: Shut up, I'll dress you in a flour sack if you give me any lip.

ARTHENICE: Let us exercise self-control for they have lost their minds. We have a proclamation to draw up, let's get it ready.

MRS SORBIN: Let's. *(To* LINA.*)* And you, wait here until the men leave their Council meeting, Don't talk to Persinet if he comes by, whatever you do. Promise?

LINA: Yes, mother.

MRS SORBIN: And let us know the minute the men show up, right away.

*(*MRS SORBIN *and* ARTHENICE *exit.* LINA *is left alone.)*

LINA: What a to-do! What a mess! Will I ever get married at this rate? I can't see my way clear.

(Enter PERSINET.*)*

PERSINET: Well, Lina, dearest Lina, let me know how bad things are. Why does Mrs Sorbin drive me away? I'm quaking like a leaf, I'm at my wit's end, I'm at death's door.

LINA: Oh my! This dear little man, if only I could speak to him in his affliction.

PERSINET: Well, you can, I'm not on another planet.

LINA: But I'm not allowed, they don't want me even to look at you, and I'm sure they're spying on me.

PERSINET: What! You turn away from me?

LINA: Still, he can talk to me, they didn't tell me to stop him.

PERSINET: Lina, dear Lina, why do you stand a mile away? Unless you take pity on me, I'm not long for this world. Right now I need a glance to keep me alive.

LINA: But if, as it happens, only a glance can save my Persinet, oh! whatever mother may say, I won't let him die.

*(*LINA *looks at* PERSINET.*)*

PERSINET: Ah! the ideal remedy! I feel life returning. Do it again, m' love, one more glance from your fair orbs to put me on my feet.

LINA: And if one glance isn't enough, I'll give you two, three, as many as you need. *(She looks at him.)*

PERSINET: Ah! I'm feeling a bit better. Now tell me the rest; but talk closer and not as if I'm somewhere else.

LINA: Persinet isn't aware that we are in a state of rebellion.

PERSINET: Rebellion against me?

LINA: And that government policy stands in our way.

PERSINET: Eh! What are they up to?

LINA: And that the women are resolved to rule the world and make the laws.

PERSINET: Am I stopping them?

LINA: He doesn't know that any minute we are going to be ordered to give up men.

PERSINET: But not boys?

LINA: That we will be ordered to be ugly and frumpy when men are around for fear they will take pleasure in seeing us, and all this by means of a proclamation to the blare of a trumpet.

PERSINET: Well, I challenge all the trumpets and all the proclamations in the world to keep you from being pretty.

LINA: And that I must stop wearing pumps or a corset, my bonnet will be back to front and I may be dressed in a flour sack: can you imagine what I'll look like.

PERSINET: Always yourself, my darling.

LINA: But the men are coming out, I'll slip away to warn my mother. Ah! Persinet! Persinet! *(She runs off.)*

PERSINET: Wait, now I see. Ah! blasted laws, I'll complain to these gentlemen.

(Enter MR SORBIN, HERMOCRATES, TIMAGENES, *another* MAN.*)*

HERMOCRATES: No, Lord Timagenes, we could not make a better choice. The commoners have no objection to Mr Sorbin, the rest of the citizens were unanimous for you, and we are in the very best of hands.

PERSINET: Gentlemen, let me appeal to you. You especially, Mr Sorbin. Government policy is cutting my throat, I'm crushed. You think you've got a son-in-law but you're wrong. Mrs Sorbin has ordered my retreat until peace is declared. You've been sent packing too, they want nothing to do with our sort of person, every male face is banished. They're going to do away with us to the blare of the trumpet, and I request your protection from the uprising.

MR SORBIN: What do you mean, my son? What uprising?

PERSINET: A riot, a conspiracy, a revolt, a hulla-balloo over governing the nation. You know the women have sworn to be ugly, to do away with slippers, there's even talk of changing their clothes and wearing sackcloth, and putting their bonnets on lopsided to make us miserable. I watched them organize a big talkfest. I moved the benches myself to facilitate their discussion. I tried to sit down, they chased me away as if I were a Peeping Tom. The world is going to rack and ruin, and all because of your laws that these fine ladies want to make in partnership with you. And I advise you to let them take on half of it, as is only fair.

TIMAGENES: Is what he's saying possible?

PERSINET: What do laws matter? They're mere trifles compared to the endearments of ladies!

HERMOCRATES: Begone, young man.

PERSINET: What's wrong with them? All anybody ever says is Get out. It's beyond me. *(He exits.)*

MR SORBIN: So that's what they were trying to tell us before?

TIMAGENES: Apparently.

HERMOCRATES: Fortunately, the escapade is more comic than dangerous.

ANOTHER MAN: Sure thing.

MR SORBIN: My wife is headstrong, and I'll wager she's the one who started the riot; but wait for me here. I'll go and see what's up, and put a stop to this nonsense. Once I'm in the driver's seat, I'll shut their mouths. Don't go away, gentlemen. *(He exits to one side.)*

TIMAGENES: What surprises me is that Arthenice is involved in it.

(Enter PERSINET, ARTHENICE, MRS SORBIN, *a* WOMAN *with a drum and* LINA, *holding a proclamation.)*

ARTHENICE: Gentlemen, please answer our question: you are about to frame the rules and regulations for the Republic. Are we to work on them together? What part do you intend us to play in this matter?

HERMOCRATES: None, as usual.

ANOTHER MAN: To put it bluntly, get married when you're girls, obey your husbands when you're wives and stick to housekeeping. We can't take that away from you, that's your lot in life.

MRS SORBIN: Is that your last word? Beat the drum: *(To* LINA*)* and you, tack up the proclamation to this tree.

(The drum is beaten and LINA *puts up the proclamation.)*

HERMOCRATES: But what's the meaning of this bad joke? Speak to them, Lord Timagenes, learn what it's all about.

TIMAGENES: Will you explain yourself, madam?

MRS SORBIN: Read the proclamation, it's self-explanatory.

ARTHENICE: It will inform you that we wish a share in everything, a partnership, to practice along with you all professions, finance, law, warfare.

HERMOCRATES: Warfare, madam?

ARTHENICE: Yes, warfare, sir. Be advised that up to now we've held back only because of our upbringing.

MRS SORBIN: Blood and thunder! If you give us weapons, we'll be more violent than you. In a month's time we should be able to flourish a pistol as deftly as a fan. A few days ago I shot at a parrot, sure as I'm standing here.

ARTHENICE: It's all a matter of practice.

MRS SORBIN: Same way, to be high-court Judge, Privy Councilor, Police Inspector, Army Captain or Lawyer.

A MAN: Female lawyers?

MRS SORBIN: Come, come, we've got the gift of gab, wouldn't you say?

ARTHENICE: I don't think you'd deny our tongues are glib enough.

HERMOCRATES: It's unthinkable. The gravity of the bench and the respectability of the bar will never accommodate a horsehair wig worn on top of a bonnet!

ARTHENICE: And just what is a horsehair wig, gentlemen? Is it more important than any other headdress? Besides, it's no more relevant to our negotiations than to your code of laws. Up to now it's been your justice and not ours; justice that does as it pleases; justice that's influenced by our bright eyes whenever we choose to look in its direction. And if we have a share in framing laws, you'll see what we'll do to that justice, as well as to the horsehair wigs which could be pig's bristles if you provoke us. Widows and orphans will be none the worse for it.

A MAN: And that's not the only thing you'll plant on our heads…

MRS SORBIN: Ah! what a wit. But once and for all, we won't budge in inch. If you think otherwise read our edict, the bottom line is your dismissal.

HERMOCRATES: Lord Timagenes, give your orders and deliver us from this caterwauling.

TIMAGENES: Madam…

ARTHENICE: Sir, I have no more to say, make the most of it. Every nation complains of the defects in its government. What is the source of those defects? They originate because the earth is deprived of our intelligence when it makes its laws, because you leave unused half of human reason, our half, and because you never apply any but your own, which is the weaker of the two.

MRS SORBIN: There you have it, not enough cloth so the gown's too short.

ARTHENICE: Men and women are united in marriage so men's ideas and ours should be united as well. The gods intended it, but the intention isn't carried out and that's the source of the law's imperfection. The universe has fallen victim to this and we assist it when we resist you. I have spoken. No answer is required. Make up your minds, we shall give you an hour, after which the rift is irreparable, unless you yield. Follow me, Mrs Sorbin, we shall go.

MRS SORBIN: *(On her way out)* Our share of intelligence bids yours a fond farewell.

(MR SORBIN re-enters as they are leaving.)

MR SORBIN: *(Stopping MRS SORBIN)* Ah! I've found you, Mrs Sorbin, I've been looking for you.

ARTHENICE: See what he wants. I shall come back for you presently. *(She exits.)*

MR SORBIN: *(To MRS SORBIN)* I'm overjoyed to see you, your carryings-on have been most amusing.

MRS SORBIN: Are they to your taste, Mr Sorbin? I'm so pleased. I'm only getting started.

MR SORBIN: You told that boy you intend to consort no longer with his sort of people. May we have a clue who you mean by that?

MRS SORBIN: Yes indeed, I mean whoever is the least like you, Mr Sorbin.

MR SORBIN: What are you saying, Mrs Bee in Her Bonnet?

MRS SORBIN: What's on my mind and what I'll stick to, Mr High Hat.

TIMAGENES: Take it easy, Mrs Sorbin. Is it fitting for a wife with your good sense to forget the respect she owes her husband?

MRS SORBIN: Hark at him, with his male rigmarole! It's just because I have good sense that things are the way they are. You say I owe him, but he owes me as well. When he pays me, I'll pay him, that exactly what I've been demanding of him.

PERSINET: Well, pay up, Mr Sorbin, pay up, let's all pay up.

MR SORBIN: Bold as brass!

HERMOCRATES: Don't you see that this venture will never succeed.

MRS SORBIN: You think we lack determination? Oh! no, no, no, our measures are taken, it's all been resolved, our bags are packed.

TIMAGENES: But where will you go?

MRS SORBIN: Straight ahead every time.

TIMAGENES: What will you live on?

MRS SORBIN: Fruits, herbs, roots, shellfish, thin air. If need be, we'll fish, we'll hunt, we'll turn into savages, and our life will end in honor and glory and not in the absurd humility in which you want to keep persons of our caliber.

PERSINET: And who are the objects of my admiration.

HERMOCRATES: This is bordering on madness. *(To* MR SORBIN*)* Give her an answer.

MR SORBIN: What do you want? It's some kind of mania, but let's get down to earth. Do you know, Mrs Sorbin, the stuff I'm made of?

MRS SORBIN: Hark at that! The poor man with his stuff. Stuff and nonsense is what he means. Pure drivel!

MR SORBIN: Drivel! Who are you talking to, may I ask? Am I not the people's choice? Am I not your husband, your master, and head of the household?

MRS SORBIN: You're this, you're that... You think you'll make me quake with this inventory of your titles which I know better than you? I advise you to watch your step. Why, doesn't he make it sound like he's lord of creation? You've been elected by the men, and I by the women; you're my husband, I'm your wife; you're the master, and I'm the mistress. When it comes to head of the household, easy does it, it's got two heads, you're one, and I'm the other, we're even.

PERSINET: Her words are pure gold, honest to goodness.

MR SORBIN: However, a woman's respect…

MRS SORBIN: In the first place, respect is an ass. Let's be done with this, Mr Sorbin, people's choice, husband, master and head of the household. That's all fine and dandy; but listen to me once and for all, you'd better. Let's say the world is a farm, the gods overhead are the landlords, and you men, since the dawn of time, have always been the farmers all by yourselves, and that's not fair. Give us our share of the farm. You govern, we govern; you obey, we obey. Let's share the profit and loss. Let's be farmers and farm hands in common. Do this, wife; do that, husband. That's the way it should go, that's the mold in which we must cast the laws, we want it, we intend it, we're set on it. Don't you want it? I hereby proclaim and make known to you that your wife, who loves you, who you should love, who is your companion, your dear friend and not your little maid-servant, unless you are her little man-servant, I make it known to you that she is your property no longer, she is leaving you, breaking up the happy home and handing you back the house keys. I have spoken for myself. My daughter is standing by, I shall call her and she shall speak for herself. Come over here, Lina.

(*Enter* LINA)

MRS SORBIN: I've said my piece, say yours, give us your opinion about the way things stand.

LINA: My opinion, mother…

TIMAGENES: The poor child is trembling at what you're making her do.

MRS SORBIN: Right you are, she's only a child. Be bold, my girl, speak up and enunciate.

LINA: Mother dear, my opinion is, as you've said, we are ladies and mistresses on an equal footing with these gentlemen. Let us work as they do to frame the laws, and then let us, as the saying goes, draw the short straw to see which one will be king or queen. Otherwise, let each one go his or her own way, us to the right, them to the left, as best we can. Is that all of it, mother?

MRS SORBIN: Are you forgetting the clause about lovers?

LINA: That's the toughest to memorize. You still insist that love is an ass.

MRS SORBIN: We're not asking for my opinion, but yours.

LINA: Oh dear! Mine is to take my lover and our love along with us.

PERSINET: What a kind heart, what a beautiful instinct for loving.

LINA: Yes, but I've been ordered to bid you a farewell which has no end.

PERSINET: Mercy!

MR SORBIN: Heaven help us. Tell the truth, is this any way to live, wife?

MRS SORBIN: Let's go, Lina, make one last curtsey to Mr Sorbin who is now a stranger to us, and let's be off without a backward look.

(They exit.)

PERSINET: That separation is my death sentence, I won't make it to supper-time.

HERMOCRATES: You seem on the verge of tears, Mr Sorbin?

MR SORBIN: I'm beyond that, Lord Hermocrates, I'm over the verge.

PERSINET: If you want to see splendid tears of the largest size, take a look at mine.

MR SORBIN: I love those flibbertigibbets more than I thought. We've got to fight and that's not my way of doing things.

TIMAGENES: I don't blame you for relenting.

PERSINET: Who doesn't love the fair sex?

HERMOCRATES: Leave us, little man.

PERSINET: You're the most pig-headed of the lot, Lord Hermocrates. Here's Mr Sorbin the best-natured man there is. Here's me who's as broken-hearted as you could wish. Here's Lord Timagenes who thinks there's nothing wrong with compromise. No one's being a wild beast, you're the only one showing his claws, and if it weren't for you, we'd share the farm.

HERMOCRATES: Hold on, gentlemen, we can come to an accommodation, if you wish it, and since you don't care for violent solutions. I've just had an idea. Will you trust me?

TIMAGENES: All right, act in our name, we give you full authority.

MR SORBIN: And even my public trust too, if I'm allowed.

HERMOCRATES: Run, Persinet, call them back, make haste, they aren't far.

PERSINET: Oh! sure thing, I'll go like the wind, I'll race like a yearling.

HERMOCRATES: And be sure to bring me a little table and writing implements at the same time.

PERSINET: Right away. *(Exits)*

TIMAGENES: Would you like us to withdraw?

HERMOCRATES: Yes, but since we are waging war against the savages of this island, come back in a little while and tell us that they've been seen coming down from their mountains in great numbers and are moving to attack us. Just that. You may also bring with you a few men bearing arms and present them as battle-ready.

(PERSINET *returns with a table, on which are ink, paper and a quill.*)

PERSINET: *(Putting down the table)* Those divine creatures are right on my tail, and this is for your writing, Mr Notary. Try to scribble your notes on this piece of paper.

TIMAGENES: Let's go.

(MR SORBIN, TIMAGENES *and* PERSINET *exit.* MRS SORBIN *and* ARTHENICE *enter.*)

HERMOCRATES: *(To* ARTHENICE*)* You have won the day, madam, you triumph over a resistance which would deprive us of the joy of living with you, a resistance which would not have been of long-standing if all the women in the colony were like noble Arthenice. Her reasoning, her refinement, her graces and her breeding would quickly have won us over. But to speak frankly, the character of Mrs Sorbin, who is to share with you the authority to enact laws, made us hesitant at first—not that we do not think her a woman worthy in her own way, but the lowness of her status, which usually implies vulgar behavior, so I'm told…

MRS SORBIN: Mercy me! This low character with her low status…

HERMOCRATES: These are not my words, I am saying what people think. They even add that Arthenice,

refined as she is, must be at some pains to stoop to
your level.

ARTHENICE: *(Aside, to* HERMOCRATES*)* I advise you not
to irritate her.

HERMOCRATES: As for me, I accuse you of nothing,
I take it on myself to tell you on behalf of those
gentlemen that you shall have a share in all branches
of government and I am ordered to draw up the act in
your presence. But, before I begin, think if you have
anything else in particular to demand.

ARTHENICE: I object to only one article.

MRS SORBIN: And so do I. There is one I don't like, and
I want it struck out. It's the one about the nobility. I
would delete it and do away with the idea of upper
and lower classes and all that rubbish.

ARTHENICE: What, Mrs Sorbin, you would do away
with the nobility?

HERMOCRATES: I also approve of that deletion.

ARTHENICE: You, Hermocrates?

HERMOCRATES: Sorry, madam, I have two little reasons
for it. I am both middle-class and a free-thinking
philosopher.

MRS SORBIN: Both your reasons will be taken into
account. I order, by virtue of my full authority, that
the individuals Arthenice and Sorbin will be equal and
that it will be as honorable to be named Hermocrates
or Fiddle-de-dee as Timagenes. How can a name confer
distinction?

HERMOCRATES: Verily, she argues like Socrates.
Consent, madam, I am about to write it down.

ARTHENICE: I shall never consent to that. I was born
with a privilege I shall keep, if you please, Madam
Market Basket.

MRS SORBIN: Eh! Come, come, comrade, you're too smart to be a snob.

ARTHENICE: Show off the vulgarity you're accused of!

MRS SORBIN: Shut your mouth, you remind me of a baby crying for its rattle.

HERMOCRATES: Take it easy, ladies, let us leave this article to one side, we can come back to it.

MRS SORBIN: Say what yours is, My Lady High-and-Mighty Deputy.

ARTHENICE: It's rather more sensible than yours, Sorbin. It concerns love and marriage. Any act of infidelity dishonors a woman. I want men to be treated the same way.

MRS SORBIN: No, that makes no sense and I veto it.

ARTHENICE: What I say makes no sense?

MRS SORBIN: No sense at all, less than none.

HERMOCRATES: I choose not to agree with you on that score, Mrs Sorbin. I find the proposal fair enough, man though I am.

MRS SORBIN: I won't have it. A man does not have our will-power. I sympathize with his frailty. Society has given him free rein when it comes to fidelity and I won't take it away from him. That's the only way he knows to behave to us women. As for us, our infidelity doesn't shame us enough. Therefore I order the dose to be doubled. The more shame we have, the more honorable we shall be, the more appreciated will be the splendor of our virtue.

ARTHENICE: She's raving mad!

MRS SORBIN: Well, I'm talking like a woman of low status. You see, we lower-class women, we don't swap lovers or husbands, whereas upper-class ladies are different, they play fast and loose with decency and behave like men. But my legislation will put them in their place.

HERMOCRATES: What do you say to that, madam, and what am I to write?

ARTHENICE: Eh! How can a person law-make with this fishwife?

(Enter TIMAGENES, MR SORBIN *and a few* MEN *bearing arms.)*

TIMAGENES: *(To* ARTHENICE*)* Madam, a great horde of savages has been spotted coming down to the plain to attack us. We have already assembled the men. Hasten for your part and Mrs Sorbin's to assemble the women and order them to commence military manoeuvers. We have brought you these weapons.

MRS SORBIN: I appoint you colonel in this matter. The men will still be in command until we've learned the ropes.

MR SORBIN: But at least come and do battle.

ARTHENICE: This woman's brutality makes me disgusted with the whole affair. I renounce a project that cannot be achieved if she's involved.

MRS SORBIN: Her silly vainglory reconciles me with you lot. Come on, husband, I forgive you. Go and fight, I'll look after your household.

TIMAGENES: I am delighted to see the matter settled. Fear not, ladies. Go and seek shelter from the war. And when we come to frame the constitution of our society we shall be mindful of your rights.

END OF PLAY

Printed in the USA
CPSIA information can be obtained
at www.ICGtesting.com
LVHW021546141123
763927LV00001B/181

9 780881 459111